IN THE MUSEUM OF
LEONARDO DA VINCI

For Mark and Lyn

IN THE MUSEUM OF
LEONARDO DA VINCI

and Alayna

Jeffrey Round

Jeffrey Round

TIGHTROPE BOOKS

Tightrope Books
167 Browning Trail
Barrie, Ontario. L4N 5E7
www.tightropebooks.com

Editor: Keith Garebian
Copy editor: Deanna Janovski
Cover design: Deanna Janovski
Typography: Dawn Kresan
Author photo credit: Don McNeill

Printed and bound in Canada

We thank the Canada Council for the Arts, the Ontario Arts
Council, and the Government of Ontario through the book pub-
lishing tax credit for their support of our publishing program.

Library and Archives Canada Cataloguing in Publication

Round, Jeffrey, author
In the Museum of Leonardo da Vinci / Jeffrey Round.

Poems. ISBN 978-1-926639-78-9 (PBK.)

    1. Leonardo, da Vinci, 1452-1519—Poetry. I. Title.

PS8635.O862515 2014   c811'.54   C2014-903071-1

For my father, Leonard,
who is a logophile like me

"Painting is poetry that is seen rather than felt, and poetry is painting that is felt rather than seen."

"A painter should begin every canvas with a wash of black, because all things in nature are dark except where exposed by the light."

—Leonardo da Vinci

CONTENTS

EXHIBIT I
THE HALL OF KNOWLEDGE

EXHIBIT II
SACRED GEOMETRY

EXHIBIT III
FAMILY PLOTS

EXHIBIT IV
EXPERIMENTAL BOTANY

EXHIBIT V
SINGING MACHINES

EXHIBIT VI
WAR MACHINES

EXHIBIT VII
LEONARDO IN MILAN

THE HALL OF KNOWLEDGE

Time and the Nature of Being

one cool cloud
suspended
    between two birds
soaring   etherwards
would rather be elsewhere
    not hanging
        up
        above
a sombre piazza
in northern Italy
questioning
        solid
        blue
        sky
would rather be in
    Madrid
    New York
    or even Calgary
not here, in this sere
where all eventually
        dissolves
        dissipates
    disappears
without
warning

the sun sets
the birds fly north
vanishing

the cloud is a heart
caught between
                two
                places
in time

In the Day, We

I

In the day, we
    begin
work mounts
dust gathers
and there are always windows to be cleaned
nothing shines as it used to
when children leapt at shadows
and every door opened onto the street

Some things stay clean

In this place
golden orbs glide along staircase
                balustrades
ferns drip from
atop the bookcases (like the essence of
an essence, Dalí speaking on Dalí)

In this caged tranquillity I have seen
slight reverberations cause
monumental disasters
In this room a bell peals
and cracks widen perceptibly

a slight tremor   a door ajar
can lead to repercussions
beyond knowing

At noon we are ready
striding into the garden
our nakedness runs raw on the rocks.
Afterwards, in renewed serenity, we
compose ourselves
fragile with memory

II

In my garden
a faun leaps
falling like crystal
on the ground
blossoms quiver in stirring breeze
thickets mount

Memories lie scattered on the grass
           Memento mori
moving with a timorousness befitting
their delicate past

Silk snowflakes
buffet our wounded eyes
We have seen beyond what there is to see

Splendid bluebirds dive, pluck seed,
veer off
    new melons
fall ripe at our feet, sap oozing
from gouges in the flesh
this terrible jungle, this tangible dream
    of our lives
opening
    Vegetable mori

        III

In the day, we
    begin
work mounts
dust gathers
we, the unknowing, searching the unknown

In this new land feverish with emotion
some things stay clean

Accident

it is funny   how
it always seems to be
the one it is not
and one who is not intended
turns out to be
saviour   new messiah
burnished bride

how one who was friend
shows up at the end
rifle barrel tucked into belt
blood-stained boot laces
queer grin on unfamiliar face
with signs of   something
not there   when last
you saw it

somewhere   always
    someone is
who is not

underneath the rug
covers pulled back
reveal the diamond mine
the rainbow

covered in dust
centuries of concealment
disclosed in a second

worlds in tiny bubbles
float through hands
that never know the colours of a day

it is perception

and all at once
you discover something
like yourself
fragile, elusive
the voice on a tape
a slender action upheld
in fields of motion
waves of sound
a scheduled accident   borne
          on airwaves

the reel   over
tattered tape ends flap
on a revolving spindle
flap
    flap
            flap

motions slow
sounds die
echoes crash in empty shells
and everywhere   dust
     is   falling
covering   everything
as all at once
you begin to   discover
that perhaps
       perhaps
you never
           will be

Cracking

The moon says its dark prayer, fog
on water, old Indian face haunting us.

Sad as a flung glove, it hovers, watching.
Whose pool is this I lean to?

We have always known it, like faces
at a bus terminal, known and yet unknown.

Sad song, old humdrum song-singer,
rag picker of the sky. No clouds await

us this evening. Unwitting, we're turned
away, two faces under a sea of glass.

In an instant, the crush of wind on leaves
and the trees are a city of ruin.

Our hands glow empty. Madness hangs
like a scent in the air. Our throats

are full of ungodly noise.
Someone could suffocate us.

Your face fades in the dusk, an ash portrait
hovering out of reach

like a field of lost promise. There is
nothing between us now. Light fails,

catches on the sound of branches snapping
in the wind. The moon is hollow and

hard like a heart. Already,
we barely exist.

Flown (For Anne Michaels)

(On the Death of Athos—on Viewing Jeremy Podeswa's
Fugitive Pieces)

Though I hold your hand in my hand
and press my fingers against your back
to feel the coarse grey cloth of your sweater,
secure where it bruises my fingertips,
the tea spilled across these solitary pages
is like a hand reaching outward or a
bird flying past my window,
telling me you've already gone.

Vacation Incident

say
    you are in a small town
looking for the beach
you know it was there once
ages beyond a dream
mother's kerchief sailing
the wind   safe
in father's knowledge
there is something disconcerting now
in buildings grown small
revealing only   colour
bright red richness that was
not a dream
the people are gone, too
as if a memory has been depopulated
on every corner shrubs shrink
winding streets do not follow
the map
though your mind
says it was here
    once

the calm is deceiving
the most casual incident
speaks change
       a stone overturned

heralds the end of an era
heart skips a beat
jumps like a spider
on the underside of a rock
there is something
                gone
in a swish of black legs

it is august
on the shoulders of the sea
a perfect day
the rocks form endless chips
along the shore
sun glistening
at the edge
and you find
you have come beyond the reef
past rippling tides
now there is another spider
waiting on the rocks
smaller   bizarre
like
        things in a dream
a ladybug deposits herself
in the space between your toes
the tide comes in and goes out
        comes in and goes out

an accident on the beach
proves
you are on the right track
as you stare at the sky
for a signal to begin
like a film you
have come to see
for the second time only
the ending has changed
the best actress is missing
the one who swayed in the wind
near the top of the cliff
you knew it was her
by the way she leaned to the edge

she has been replaced
by someone with a handkerchief
waving bravely over the surf
   does not fit the scene
clashes
      with the rocks
you cannot find the colours of your dream
the face of a landscape
has changed

SACRED GEOMETRY

Arc of the Diver

you stand
poised   silence
on the diving board
arms   perfect sphere
above

                    your head
perfect
        each
naked   drop
lubricating   skin
speaks
the graceful curve
flesh   calculated
precisely to make more
of what you are:

quintessential diver

turn your head   to see
            who is watching
first   profile
then the other
till all falls into place
when you
            make perfect
dive, arc, love

yet
    in the end
you are left standing
face turned to shore
   a little colder
arms still in place
  o, artless diver
in effortless dive from high places
   you do not
               dive
do not let
    the crystal shimmering
water splash
      on neck and thighs
at cold depths
like the duck
that will not get its feathers
            wet

your art
      deco diving pose
has turned to stone
along with your queries:
"Is it moderate, temperate, wise?"
and all your loves
   are weary sighs
into the safety   of solitude

White Ice

        winter
             shards memory
          like crystal in my
        veins
dull   diapason
        of sound
           an
        old   sermon
    hanging in the air
        thunder in my ear
   sweet ear
        a crack for the dying

        I search   for signs
of damage   rough edges
        a wearing at the shoreline

      where have I been?

            sometimes in the night
        hoarfrost on   windows
       leaves   noiseless
pictures of passing
        on my morning pillow
            tearstains like
                            tiny

pinpricks of blood

is it madness
                          I am come upon
or simply   the season?
                  what keeps me treading
horizons
                          heavy with fear
thin ice under evening sky
            instead of foraging open
                                    distance

            skating over the   surface
                    of this   brief
            love-locked existence?

Becoming Planet

Somewhere out there

vacant planets whirl
            hourglasses
cartwheels
                        Ferris wheels
spinning out
concentric logic
      in realms beyond

with a camera's sharp click
   eternity comes into
                        focus
         briefly

   as we become dust
particles of change
turn into
            building blocks
         light   beams
carry us

past star patterns
spangled across
                  universes

ferry pieces of us to
          other
planets   galaxies
out there

in the
                    deep
unknowable space
between stars
will we be
          re-named
Ursa Minor   Alpha Centauri
          Omega

After the Storm

afterwards we walk in white
the weight of sky,
while
texture of grey cloud breath
   reveals damage
change
                 betrayal
in secret places
walls   hidden
beneath clotted strands of snow

a blanket of barbed wire
woven into hearts
covers   regret
like the aftermath of a funeral
      open ground
            naked space
sounds of shovels chucking,
gravel thrown high
into the air
     catch me

          I'm falling

we move slowly
toward separate gates
nonchalant, lingering
feigning interest
                in branches
fallen   on paths as though
hurrying from   nothing
nowhere to go in all this
        empty space
staring up from
        the bottom
                of a pit

In Praise of Art

(Fragments from the End of Time…)

I

there is a time
when
            things
unconscious
of their own existence
elbowing their way
past   me
(I stand like a guardian in time)
to the fore
become more
than   trinkets
lost in the stonecutter's dust

II

a point   at which
still
    life becomes more
than mere art
revolving
around this pedestal of distractions
floundering in space

III

synchronicity is explained
as polarized
                existence
between two places in time
the final solution
is not
        dying

IV

when church doors open
 'holy, holy, holy'
they beckon to you
call
this time seething with experience
you seize the call
shower the halls with darkness
stained glass
soothes the mind
imminently finer

V

a word is found
and broken broke

a blossom
a seal
touching nothingness
the unknowing untouchableness

VI

there is a time
when time
elbowing past
at such a pace
will wipe the
sculptor's grin from
his unrepentant brow
besmirch his head with
soot and ash
holy to the universe

VII

this problem
of existence
beside a starry void
plagues our eyes
and drives us
Cain-like to
        far shores
fearful of the destiny

             to which time
marches
        sealing fates like
candies in a jar
(this being in time/
      this time when things
being)

                VIII

a great body of
souls
moving forward
at too great a pace
dreaming of a
motionless
forever
beside
the invisible stream

                IX

a landscape
an architectural dream
with human figures
well lit, but not altogether obtrusive
dissolving in the background

Two Views of Heiligkreuz

Dusk

Evening clouds brim over the
valley like a mirror of solitude,
saint-like peaks inclining above,
islands set adrift in a stream of fog.

Black forest tapestries bead into night.
Tail lamps wink like fish silver,
fall over the edge, gleaming under
dark waters, silent fields.

The moon is buried under vines.
Only the church spire illumines,
still and solitary as an overturned cup,
a surprising lighthouse, pale

beneath black glass, cold water.
Bells toll the hour and the evening
is as lost as sheep in fog.
Night swallows the lights

in the valley one by one,
like waves over-running the shore.
The horizon of mountains lingers,
stone Babel, then quickly withdraws

without a sigh. Village lights blink
and churn, drowning constellations
ten-thousand leagues under the sea,
great mother, eternal blackness.

Dawn

Below these hills of dark relief,
through beaded towns
on a diminutive tapestry, trains
move slow like a procession

of crucifixes, unstitching darkness
into little pearls of light.
Sunday worshippers climb the barren
fields like stones labouring

toward illumination or grey piétas
gathering in the true altitude
for a communion of absolutes.
Below, stalking cold-solitary figures

happen upon Stations of the Cross,
a relay for paralytics or the blind,
the green, unmapped progress of pilgrims
measured by ancient prayer.

In litany of stone, wind, dead branches,
amid immaculate wilderness of diamond peaks,
the sun breaks over the hills as morning
inches forward like a slowly opening wound.

Heiligkreuz (*The Holy Cross*) is a Swiss village 31 kilometres outside
Lucerne, with a ski lift, a sixteenth-century hotel (in which these poems
were written), and one of the world's most famous Roman Catholic
churches. A piece of wood said to be from the cross carried by Jesus Christ
to Golgotha is preserved and displayed on its altar. On Good Friday, an
annual pilgrimage occurs with hundreds of worshippers climbing the
mountain in a re-enactment of Christ's procession to his crucifixion.

The Silver Cord

("Or ever the silver cord be loosed…" Ecclesiastes 12:6-7)

Only traces   content of inner sounds
          keys   broken
                    buoy up the mast
the mainstay holds but barely for now
seize the capstan, constant swelling of our oceans
                    miles away
it is a season and a sign all at once
there is drifting and the occasional rush of wind
to charge the ballast with floating then
drift open-ward till we can enter the new solution

Fast foaming all around us everywhere as at the
centre of a bubble   where everything is
one way and many, too vast to hold
such precious warmth in   hands
there is   no looking back
by way of reasoning though heart be wrought with
open degrees, leagues, latitudes, but now is not
to be   followed
beyond this sign post   some things fly past
others pulled behind, cut off from earth like a rocket
leaving its orbit in stages

Here is no more falling only the drifting within
as we enter   remark
the constant rising up everywhere

FAMILY PLOTS

Mothers

when I was, say
three,
my mother, thinking I
should share in the accumulated
wisdom of the ancients,
taught me the earth is round
not knowing
I would test her theory
being curious

at the edge of a cliff
I slid to the valley floor below
landing face downwards in snow,
frightened but unhurt, I
scrambled
      back to the top

she kept me inside all day
I could not go to
the movies as promised
tales of warriors and lost lands
perhaps fearing I would test
another of her theories
of time and three dimensions
vanishing off-screen
amid reports by astonished patrons

that a small boy was last seen
clad in dried skins, sword
unsheathed, scabbard hanging
at his side, fighting off dinosaurs
running across horizons, wild
a cry tearing from his throat

mothers change slowly
worlds revolve around them
while they remain
more or less the same
for eons
even now
she has not changed:
                    hair like frost
                skin cracking like dried earth
        eyes sharp as stars
and the vast universe of her being
swallowing me   with
dinosaurs and mountain peaks

at thirty   I am
the age she was
when I was born
the earth has moved round her
twice thirty
but here she is still:

                        house gone, children grown
                    apartment complex
                crystallizing round her
over-run with small white-haired gnomes
a mythic race, fair and slow moving
remembered from some film I had seen
when I was, say
five

at the gate we meet
wandering onto the grounds
of her fabled, her lost lands
scarf tied round neat wisps of grey
hands, cool dress
                flowering in the breeze
we wander across fields
laughing as the wheat
grows up round our waists
                not far from here
is the cliff I fell from
the valley I discovered with my fall
the dinosaurs must be very near, I know
so I was not far off after all

we part, as mother and child
                                        do
I leave her standing on the grounds
and move away

from this new found land
so quickly, so easily
after having discovered it
                    at last

as I walk away, I turn
to call her name, but
the wind catches my breath
and I hold it
like a lark turning

I look for her turning
a signal, some sign
that I will be with her
when she walks off-screen
across the horizon to the dinosaurs
from where I stand
                    I
cannot distinguish her among tall
stalks of flowers
head bowed, cool dress blowing
                    in the wind
now standing still
        now moving
toward the edge

Playground

'beat … beat'

then my uncle seeing where I sat
breaking stone on stone for amusement
called me, his voice gruff,
come with me, boy, to this place
I climbed up in him so high
big in his pick-up with the slippery seats
red lady swinging from the mirror
I said I thought I could see heaven
we were so high
where's that? he said
I knew then we were going
to another place, different skies

we took the old, round fridge with us
in the back of the truck
like a giant snowman
rumbling on to a place, somewhere
off the highway past great slabs
of pine, juniper and trees I could not name
under tunnels of leaves
hanging, over bumps
the truck leaving earth
on certain spots

till we came out the mountain
top like a graveyard
for fridges and stoves

we stopped and put ours in a row
with three others, one blue
I found a seagull's feather
beside the path and showed Uncle Joe
who said it was magical,
it did not come from any bird
then he put it in his stove-pipe hat
and danced a blind man's jig
to the radio blaring in the pick-up
Elvis Presley and some song about a dog
crying over the collected garbage
I found a fiddle near a burning mound
and started to *squawk, squawk, squawk*
with a pine branch for my bow

I felt drunk with the madness in my blood
I heard my aunt talking about to a neighbour
Uncle Joe just kept dancing with a blind man's fervour
the world turning like a kaleidoscope
in dirty, blistering hands
earth going one way
and sky moving another
till the ground under me was changing, too
mountain tops of garbage swaying
over the smouldering crater of earth

I sprawled out in the back of the truck
the sky riding at me like birds in fright
at the hunter's approach
pictures of brides and weddings
going through my head
flowers descending on earth
I thought of my mother—did she love me,
was she happy where no man could beat her?
then the sky fell off into darkness
and we rumbled home in the stumbling dusk

and now I rumble on to where I am going
a place I have seen before, sometimes
on starry nights, beside the highway
scanning horizons in clear, clear visions
passing a lighted home along the roadside
I leave my history behind
in the bourn of these old, warm houses
on the shore of distances
too far to cover in a lifetime
I see this place
playground for the poor and young
where an old man wearing a wigwam
dances a blind man's jig
a place where stone feathers beat
hand on hand, making a sound
like a heart in the darkness

Pink Lady

I am a pink lady in a red dress
a yellow parasol hoisted above
to confound the sun
my thighs are white and thick
my ankles girders attached to beams
from this height I could hoist
my belongings up in winches

My husband dawdles beside me
focused on his own little world,
sullen oyster on an unappetizing shell,
we suffer the real one badly
like two fools who have come to the fair
and mistake the flying trapeze
for the dancing bear

We step along, dragging feet
in the mud of our discontent
(he wishes I were prettier—so do I
I wish he were richer—so does he)
stifling small chagrins
to stop and admire finery in windows:
lovely shoes, a fine dress I cannot wear
and he cannot afford

When I was a girl, daddy promised
me love and happiness always
(he was foolish, brave and kind)
I believed him then
so when I became a woman
I found a man who resembled him
and fell in step behind

Soft regrets flower round us now
wreathed in gentle melancholy,
we have only each other to blame
as we wander half-heartedly
down steaming streets
looking at life in shop windows
wishing to be anything other
than what we are

Cold Comfort

in this room, crucifixes
stare like the eyes of the dead
my grandmother is laid out
in violet lace and white satin,
filled with a cold that numbs
the bone, while I wait for the
breath that gives warmth to
return a virgin's blush to those
cheeks, a touch of summer
in dead winter

I sit on a chair, wooden back
intricately carved handles, a
seat too hard for comfort
or the ease intended by it
as relatives pour by like lead
to reassure themselves
her battles are really over
and did they remember
to thank her for everything?

this room wears its grief
like a crown of thorns,
not unlike the room
my grandmother sat

in for forty years, mending
socks, watching telly,
having a laugh and a
game of cards with the kids
waiting for the knock
that never came, the sound
of footsteps that did not
return to the warm interior
like hope or need, where
the faithful await
the miracle of a god
whose glance means
you might disappear
and never come again

as must have
happened to my grandfather
on battlefields of glory
waving his flag high, felled
in one sure stroke
and gone to a greater mansion
than this tawdry place
he called home

Arrangements

(*For Dawn Rae Downton and all the herbal tea on Robie Street*)

this
      is how it stands:

in the kitchen you have left
               a cup
          on the lip
of the table
               a kettle
near my sideboard
          whistles longingly
after you
        till I ease
               its calling

I let a spoon   stray
      by the window
for hours
          when you left
(I hadn't the heart
          to call it back)

milk stains
               the counter
attest to your presence
layers left
        behind

to remind me
                    the delicacy
of arranging
the sugar and cream
            of daily living

things linger
        bric-a-brac
                    on shelves
recalling   places

we have been

the half-life of a teapot
whispers
                    of happier times
starker arrangements
            of settings
spoon, knife, napkin
        to the fore
a side plate
                    all these things
        in place
except you, whose absence
        is everything

in this arrangement
        tact and formality
tear and strain

              the tissues of living
this   is not
                            the way
I thought it would be

blue-green grass
on a china lawn
              stuffed doll waving
                          in the window

if I were
              a flower arranger
it would all be
              perfect
                          tomorrow

Beggar

Sad Father,
I have known thee
these thirty years
a-changing.
Old Nasty,
miser-mister
thy cry
a token
dumb-show.

Cardboard foot,
empty-bag man
you scared
my children
a-boogie dreaming
in grey ash houses
with blood hands,
vile smiles
these many-an-hour.

A thank-you, good day
to all who come
clattering, hands held out
or niggard-drawn
fingers sewn into pockets

like a scallop penny
give-a-way.

No luck today, hoarder
thy pockets empty,
house a trash heap
your bags a rainbow,
cornucopia of dreaming.

Mr. No-pillow,
Thin-blanket,
this wad's too
hard of hearing,
too shy of giving
a shiny penny
for Poor Tom.

Cry you mercy,
Poor Tom's a-cold!

Wednesday Morning Launderette

the socks of a god
are not like these
not refined
square checks on black holes
drifting off into clouds
representing eternity

Dionysus
would not wear wool
except on religious holidays
even then
it was not combed through
more than once

twice is too often
for such holy ones

Mercury would wear Nikes now
or something with a buffalo on it
representing playfulness
of the godly life
wine and orgies lasting
for weeks on end
no wars now
in 21st century obsolescence

my pristine manners
would not hold up there
in the space beyond
clouds

if I hold my socks up
I can see through the holes
to the space beyond
the clouds
where light dwells
pristine examples of the saintly
margin beyond margin
extracting the pure
filtering through the web and weft
flecks and fibres

caught
like little flies down here
on the mortal side of the weave
the socks of a god

are not like these

For George

(Redbone Coonhound, Neutered 21 July 1993)

You will begin to notice
an absence lately,
the falling off of some vague
indefinable excrescence,
a ticking in the veins
growing less vital
daily

It will not hurt you, will
make you more
approachable, less
defiant as the maleness
that is you subsides
into unchallenged calm
a cooling of testosteronic
plates beneath the surface
of your unruly demeanour

The timely demise of
testicular orbs, those glowing
vitals of jelly and hormone
should please you
now that your need
for cars, bicycles
tree stumps and squirrels

has likewise diminished,
a calling that kept you
up all night, made you
unrepentant, returning
home long-eared
at having yet again
jumped the fence
of your little
kingdom

Fear not, O diggy dog!
O great howler
of neighbourhood news
this throne of green
grass kingdom, fenced backyard
is your earthly doggy reward

EXPERIMENTAL BOTANY

Leaves and Laertes

Inside the magnificent cavern
       of the human heart
one strikes a vein
the way prospectors strike silver
or gold
the prisms of sunset
falling in a chimera of hope

Clarity of feeling
fades like dusk
turning, windstorm, maelstrom
winding in fury down a cliff of stone
till we lie shattered
at its face

How far have we come, these
bits of broken matter
discarded and impotent
slivers of shale in a sullen ditch

Three stars flail themselves across the
evening sky
like witches
turning a bitches' brew
of time
bitterly describing sunset for those

who are blind
to passion

Strange petals howl
a loveless sister
drowning and drowning
is half-heard in
the murmuring twilight
her words an orison to day's
wounds:

>A green thing sat
>beside me
>like a spider or
>a gnat or a mayfly
>brandishing great arms
>at me

I have a taste for the dark
it descends on me nightly
like a mantle or a spirit
a thin, grey coat of saliva

But growth means change
and leaves that blossom
must sure as fade

With a hey, and a ho,
and a hey-nonny-no!

Postcards from India

Enclosed is a leaf

Enclosed is a leaf from a Bodhi tree. Inside it lies the essence of what makes a tree a tree—different from a monkey or a whale or a human eye. In every single leaf is an entire forest just as in every drop of rain is the ocean, only not so deep. A blessing and mystery at the same time.

I also enclose my greetings, though they may not seem as endless as a leaf or a star or the sky. At Lumbini I saw a bottle labelled 'Scent of a morning from August 2, 1962.' The bottle was empty except for that captured essence, to be uncorked centuries from now when some pilgrim like me desires to know and understand what it was to be alive in August 1962, just as I have been intent on knowing what it means to breathe in the delicate scent of your being, to inhale your breath, to dance in your eyes.

The best thinking is done on foot and so the road to me is home. It is both the destination as well as the way there. I think I have never fully understood that till now. How far have I travelled to be here? How far is it still from where I am? Send me your kisses. I will bottle them and take them with me to the end of the road.

Empty bowl

I am unused to writing my thoughts down. I fear everything and putting that into words makes my fears more concrete. Well, then let me be concrete: what I fear most is losing you. A beggar with a bowl has nothing to fear because he has nothing to lose. A common enough thought, unworthy of even a postcard. But take away his bowl and see how he will squirm. An empty bowl may contain everything.

Tiger in a bush

The Way is always hidden: anger is disguised as praise, till praise becomes a silent goad. In Tantric practice, the withholding of pleasures becomes the doorway to endless delight. What is up may be down. The Way is hidden like a tiger in a bush, unseen until it springs.

Alert to all ironies, I head north to find the secret language containing worlds of possibility said to be as numerous as sand grains on the Ganges. There is rumoured to be a map leading to the unexcavated grave of every Bodhisattva.

In the meantime, here is what I know: disregard both gate and boundary. They are false and lead nowhere. Look for the sign that says "Away." When you return, it will no longer be there. Search for a passage that is both near and far, wild and calm, fearsome and soothing. Be both pirate and mendicant, lover and soldier, merchant and patron.

But first, pay your bills and lock your door. Wish your family long life and your friends great good fortune. Then pick up your begging bowl and a threadbare robe. Close your eyes, finger pointing forward, and spin. Turn your back on everything you know. Now you are ready.

All direction is inconsequential

The guide books say you must embrace an "elemental recklessness" while keeping a wary gaze on the road ahead. No matter—all direction is inconsequential. Leave your books, your journals and your poems behind. One coat is easily replaced by another. The Way exists, but where is the traveler?

Can you be charitable without being sentimental, wise without being knowing, witty without being cynical? Can you embody purity without excessive piety? Can you embrace the scorching winds of Nalanda, tolerate the bitter rains that slake no thirst, and still leave doubt behind?

Soon you will encounter the intolerable perversions of mind: whirling dervishes, the white dust of dried riverbeds, the lost dreams of kings, splendid palaces, high mountains and fearsome tigers. In time you will meet courtesans and queens, rogues and saints, poets and preachers of every kind.

The *lokapāla*, those useful deities guarding the holy sites, have performed their duty unstintingly for more than two and a half thousand years. I have marked this country end to end with the soles of my burning feet. Now I say, better to stay at home.

I have been to Bodh Gaya, Sarnath, Kusinara. Benares and Kapilavastu lie at my feet. Of all the sacred places I have known, your body is the one I remember best. Why go all that way to touch a monument of stone?

The hardest part

The hardest part of setting out is returning. It sounds contradictory, but it's true, so I'll say it again: the hardest part of setting out is returning, emptying the contents of your travelling case on the floor and saying, "This is where I have been," as though this assemblage of trinkets is the essence of all you have seen and done.

Look closely: there are no new worlds in the soiled laundry, meaningless souvenirs and scattered toiletries. Your Day-Timer is as blank as the day you left, as though time stopped while you neglected to record its passage in pages that remain empty, unlived. They can tell you nothing of where you have been.

So, I resolve to return with nothing, and take with me everything, discarding and refining myself along the way. Breathe in and breathe out. One does not hold onto the breath, but grows in and through it, before expelling it. Some things I will keep: the memory of a smile and the tears of a child, an understanding of sorrow and how over time it becomes strength, with a gleam as hard as a diamond, as colourful as a rainbow.

I will take whatever I can pack into this infinite space inside me. Don't worry. You are already there.

Making Love

sometimes
     things happen
to make me feel
       removed
from your presence
though whether it is you
or me who is less tangible
I cannot tell

the beginning
     is good
you shuck a glove
divest yourself with ease
    of coarse cotton
old skins   lie scattered
about your chair   as you
   swirl and grow
around it
things   happen
your voice grows small
lilacs   recede in your eyes
  all the while
    the faint smell
of perfume
      lingers

the light in this room
is violet
clashes   with   the colour
of petals
soft lips

you   stand
upright
vines trailing down your arms
tendrils   ensnaring
shafts of light
exploding
your fists

if I look in the mirror
at just the right angle
when we
love
I can make one of us vanish
but never
the right one

I tremble as you blossom
feel the   weight
of autumn   at my throat
dew on   lips
glistening   disappearing

till there is nothing left
but a stem
      a few leaves
these pale flowers
         scattered
at my feet

Among the Goldenrod

Here is no last hurrah
gathered in a field of amber and sullen crosses
twisted in among the sheets

Let them know it if they don't already
as they gather awkward above, afraid
of what might be seen—an eerie eyeball
or finger pointed in silent retribution
a moon-luminous fist
to drag them down into green earth

It's no picnic here, small girls
stooping to place soggy bouquets of hawthorn, nettle
floppy brim hats of shadowy finch-like ladies
their faces ancient clocks rusting in thin,
vinegary tears

The minister's threadbare voice
rattles like a bird in a battered cage
declaiming a life he knows only in death,
unrolling love from his tongue like soft
white communion wafers
is it for this we come and go?

You can smell the loam
thick and rich with the comings and goings
of matter, the stench of death rising
while they stare right through us,
each rabbit-eared one of them
lacquering us with their eyes
awaiting their leave-taking when the sorrowful carpet
is rolled back into place

Their minds run in rivulets to the future
as if returning a key to a secret room
they had been curious to see
now heading back to rows of blank-faced cars
lining the gates, thinking of meals they will eat
gifts to exchange, shiny clothes
they will wear to parties
tombstoned into their happinesses

They don't dream the moon's crookedness,
its maggoty whiteness slithering over the sky,
the wail of leaves rotting in the wind
or how it starts up again each evening
like the babble of gulls in the half light

An ashen smudge staggers across the horizon
as they turn to cut their teeth on new business
now that our absence has become a slight memory,
barely conspicuous, hardly even an embarrassment

The sun beats and beats overhead through black
branches, shadows stretched taut
while we lie like beached bones, a fish comb, bleached
and covered over, not even remembering desire,
hauled into the claw throat of this new land
drawing the sky down like a cloak,
waiting to be entered, swallowed
into this cool newness everywhere
while the mud and weeds tear
and strain all around

SINGING MACHINES

Aria

        in this, the
perfection of my love
        takes place on watching
        these hollow notes shunt
        back and forth across
        the river of clouds on
        our horizon dark with
        resentment and the
        inconstant solitude of
never having you near
        while daybreak of our season
        leads to dusk of
        discontent and never
        having you was worth
        twice the pain of loving
        you as a fading
        star on the horizon watches
        the clouds roll in never
knowing the solace
        of having been cloud
        in your eyes, nor
        star, nor daybreak
        nor dusk forming
        like a rose in
        the hollow hills of
        your brow
nor song, nor
        twilight

Valse Triste

(Sibelius at Ninety)

we have the stillness of his voice
at great pine depths, the discord of stars
                under water
winter and long nights shining

the great head nods
ponders vivid notes set against
cold seas   stark forests
the dark matter of histories receding

into the larghetto of his eyes
stone hands, stone face, mute statue
wrest from stone a little meaning

not the prolific young composer now
but an old man smouldering
through centuries of immobility

    A visitor has brought cigars from Tavastehus,
his hometown,
thick black cigars he likes so much
he chews on butt-ends like a shaman
nodding mightily
breathes smoke mightily
puffing his way through centuries, and sleeps

in the window,
upright in his favourite chair
leaving his visitor to wonder

> should he leave?
> should he speak?
> can sound disturb the dead?

cigar smoke seeping through time
through great hands that stopped their utterances
thirty years before
giving way to silence
the lid closing down on the long Finnish night

the visitor leaves
the statue wakes and sleeps

> wakes and sleeps

wrestles with the dark
falls back into the centuries closing around
hands huge, fluttering to his face
the silence huge,
thirty years

each vastness off-setting the other
like the loose ends of a symphony
coming together

> intermingling
> joining huge hands

Finnish composer Jean Sibelius (1865-1957) virtually stopped composing around 1928, producing little for the last thirty years of his life. Claiming he had nothing to offer the contemporary music world, he destroyed his own Symphony No. 8.

Barque of Metaphor (for Wallace Stevens)

out on the steps
he stands, looking up
dreams, looking up
at the woman in her room
aglow in the glare
of a naked bulb
thinking of time

feverishly strokes his head
and thinks of thousands of women
in thousands of rooms
in the glow
changing, always the same
woman

in front of him
leaves pirouette on the lawn
planes blink   overhead
heart-shaped leaves in the darkness
fill like sails in empty space

he muses how we commit our crimes
without raising a finger, shed tears
before the tragedy is mounted
in the beginning we look for the end
in winter, the transport to summer

this woman
engaged in so cruel an act
as undressing
on this bare stage room
glare of this light
she closes and goes to bed

he shivers, listens
under starry skies
car horns dominating the smell of roses
red moon under the wind
leaves dancing on lawns
blue lawns running
in every direction
catching up with the horizon
lights on hills
blinking out like rows of dominoes

the smell of roses
the red moon
the stars blinking off and on

Humpback

(*Puerto Vallarta, 3 March 2008*)

The whales leap, the sport of giants.
Flippers, huge tails smacking water,
joyful, cutting across the bay.

Blowholes snort and slash,
rending the blue-silver surface,
sending spumy shouts into the air.

Now the boats charge, sightseers cheering,
jockeying for place. The giants plunge
and dive, no use for mortal ways.

The water moves in restless eddies
above their vanished forms. As far
away as you are, you can't stop

watching, can't help wanting more.
As if the answers to life's mysteries
lay right before your eyes.

Vase by Candlelight

Consuming, consuming
the wide rift is broken
bent on concealing its origins
through a glass darkly.

Spin, spin, spinster, sister
thou'rt a flame by any other name,
light-laboured, small-waisted
o, tiny dancer.

White orchid petals enlist
thy aid, drooping tightly,
nothing else to guide their
aspiration to be bright shadow.

Sing, sing, sister lover—
ecstatic in this dance
till the wick is spent,
thy work done.

Bloor Line

What bright tumult of sound,
a fanfare for the uncommon courtiers
who sing and dance along this platform
merry, merry in their rags of mourning
all lords and ladies a-leaping

Doors thrust apart, the dance explodes,
dark atoms loosed upon the world,
multiplying and dividing their sins

A trek like no other, this
journey through trough and tunnel
over bridge and under transport beside
road and meadow greenly growing

Thrown onto morning's harsh fashion plate,
here's no feast for any man, the subway
wheels singing life's thick chug-a-lug,
the ungodly workaday rhythm,
melancholy with each swaying lurch that
brings another jostling of sulky looks
and contemptuous stares

No gods and goddesses these, but
the remnants of creation,

after-thoughts in a bedraggled couture
where the city's drabbery finds fecund state,
goading the day with sterile
contempt for life's fertile waste

Another stop,
the courtiers leap and dance anew,
drawn to this hub of great metropolis,
this grand hubbub of life, like the
once-useful drones of summer, now shucked
unwelcomed from the hive, dishonoured, loosed
directionless, upon the noble world

WAR MACHINES

Saint-Laurent-sur-Mer

Où se trouve...?

You have found the stones of Normandy—
you who drove down from the hills in your
dark grey Corso with Philip Glass
playing a soundtrack to your journey
(surprisingly appropriate for so many things).
Here you found these yellow lichen-covered stones,
where beach, sand, sea stand forevermore,
seamlessly interchanging
under the burning sun.

These stones have made their home
here, amidst the unchanging landscape
where only the tide renews itself.
At this place where a landing
marked the beginning of the end,
the slow turning of another tide,
in this place where the real tide
marbles the beach and calmness
once again prevails.

Où sont ... ? Où sont les héros
qui se sont battus
pour la gloire,

avec le courage,
à la défense du monde ?

Ils ne sont pas perdus,
mais ils restent ici
où le chant de la mer
est la chanson de Mort
et de Vie.

Pour gloire ...
pour la gloire de l'histoire.
Entre les pierres.

Here there is only a monument
and a silence like eternity.
Under the burning sun, their bones
and blood mingled with the sand and tide.
Will you stay with them here, amidst the
stones of Saint-Laurent?
What can they tell us we don't already know?
Listen. They will tell you everything.

Now, home again, a surprising second act
to your trip is about to unfold. Here,
in the laundry room, as you go about your dull
act of unfolding clothes and placing them in the washer,
a few grains of sand fall from the hem of your cuffs and
disappear quickly down the drain.

Burning, Remembering—6 December 1991

*(Candlelight vigil on the second anniversary of the
Montreal massacre)*

Finally, they are done.

Two years laboured over fourteen dead
to perfect this sheen,
this silence by vigil, by candle.

Where does memory enter?
Where does mourning begin?
From the empty womb,
a snowfall of spilt roses.
Everything is shiny,
perfect now, like tears of ice
or a smile that does
not stop.

We steal a walk of tenderness,
huddle together near flame, hand-held,
on this river of light.
The smell of grilled flesh
fills eyes and noses.
They are done. They are done.
Nothing can fill them now,
only sorrow over the old thing,
this thing done.

Even their desire is so small
it would not fill a pocket.
Is there nothing left to feed on?
No, nothing,
only the great sea—sister,
strong mother.

White-hearted, knuckle-boned,
they are newly healed,
heart-fond again.
Woman-proud, no one else
will loose or love them.

The snow is white, white
these flames are white
like paper flowers.
Our colour is sombre.
We haven't heart to go
into that whiteness.

White flames sing down
to a voiceless ash.

Rebel

(On re-viewing Nicholas Ray's *Rebel Without a Cause*)

remark
   how
 or when
   you are moved
touched
   by a
 red
 jacket
 stained t-shirt
hair comb
   slicked back
      the stars
  tapping out a beat
watching count down
   to
      fade

not knowing   when sound ends
  how lights flicker up
   like morning
 we rise   slowly
    the sun
   not to shine
   stumble to stand
  down the stairs

past the bleached-out popcorn stand
    like ruins
filtering through corridors
    of lost time

light filters through   the arched sphere
        does not us touch
    it moves away
      among the cars
      reckless teenagers
    things we cannot touch
      cannot become
      behind us

the mustachioed gentleman in blue
    pale as sky
stands
      fending off the movie's end
as something akin
      to a nervous condition
    schizophrenia
  past   present
ushers us through   portals
    to a nervous future
hesitant beat   stamped
    on empty sky

how picked-to-the-bone we feel
           afterward
as we start off   one thing
           slowly   filtered down
to become another
                standing
careless   caressless
           where
what has become isolated
are the things that inform us
      of our being
the things that matter

and find we have become
these lost objects:
     pocket comb
   stolen

                          gun

     red   jacket
place in time
           increasingly

staggering out of existence

Beggar, Midstream

He stands, head bowed,
eyes staring out and cap
held like a cup.

I've been here all day,
he moans, and I haven't
got one dollar.

The crowd's restive, foaming by
the drowning man,
avoiding his anger.

Have a good day, he says,
showering a beneficence
of nothingness on the sidewalk.

Glowering, he stands up full—
not much when all's considered—
while the steady stream of feet take

careful steps around him,
Moses dividing the waters.
Their waves break against him,

fall back onto the shore,
this sorrowful stone,
unwashed, unrepentant.

Impossible

to catch a falling star
save a stitch in time
wake the dead
re-cork a bottle
stop a runaway train
unscratch a CD
smile during *Macbeth*
drink muddy water
turn back the clock
eat my own words
mend a broken heart
ask your forgiveness
dry all your tears
lie to myself or make
you love love love
me again

Small Furies

Beware silence
distrust stillness
things that lie beneath the surface
do not seem

Death leaps up sudden
like trout from quiet water
snatching flies mid-air
or a car over-leaping the banks
of a sidewalk
pedestrians scattered
mid-stream

It's a Small World After All

My father dreamed a world that
            would make a difference
brave soldiers, free skies
    a universal anthem

Times changed, the corporations
            took over
east river dividing north
                from south

The new Hitlers wear striped shirts,
            eat hamburgers, lean against
public monuments while reciting
                    bank slogans

The people fled in droves, escaping to
            far shores—empty and silent
searching for   Nirvana
No one has heard from them since

The villains have grown so ordinary
the heroes scarcely bother them
            now
These days, even evil is hard to get right

My idols are American Idols
                British Idols
                Canadian Idols
my star is a Mega-star
(why bother with smallness anymore?)

Something
        is missing, has slipped
out of reach
it's a tragedy, but not a big one
so it doesn't count

Yesterday,
the bootblacks of Harlem struck a
                mighty chord and the
ramparts fell, but Joshua
                lay undecided
It was tea time and his omnipotence
was required elsewhere

Like my father,
I had an idea for a changing world,
a bigger, better world,
but never mind

I'm over it now.

LEONARDO IN MILAN

Last Supper

The last time we ate together you said
you wanted to know what I would do
when you left.

Is it so final, then? I asked.

I called the fortune teller the next day.
She said you were distant, not gone.
I cursed, wishing you had left for good
rather than leave pieces of me
dangling.

After a month, your e-mail arrived,
popping up on my screen. So many words,
like a spillage of stars.

In the Museum of Leonardo da Vinci

In this place,
darkness forbids us speak.
We intrude unwitting as afternoon shade,
our footsteps small with wonder.
Whose house was this?
Who wound this room full of clocks
like a cemetery of hours?

Did they listen with joy, touch
each face as the face of love?
Pipes, bottles, spindles, keys,
metal birds, chimes of glass—
each ticking sound becomes
the voice of hope.

In the room of musical instruments
notes splinter into tapestries of sound.
We're deep in sanctuaries of ignorance,
more at home here than in the light.

Who held this tender wood with care,
stroked each careful form out of silence
like a heart set free?
Someone must have loved these once, shaping
every forgotten note rising
into air like a fat silk purse.

Now, each speaks on its own:
>
> *Hear us, say the viole d'amore;*
> *Taste us, the vials of medicine;*
> *Remember us, the clocks with sad, drooping faces.*

They seize our mind, bright
with the possibility of things
far off.

What sun, what moon could illumine more?
These fingers will
span us to a new century.
Take care! they warn. Take care
you do not become too small!

In this house, the painted ceilings
and fluted walls
close in like a coffin of glass.
It is too much, too much!

How can we return to native shores, enter
old simplicities newborn?
What communion
could make such darkness light?

Where shall we put all this knowledge?
How to turn down the wick
on a lamp already out!
Geometry, astronomy, acoustics,
anatomy, duplication, memory.

Oh, my Achilles heel is aching!
It squeezes the brain like a lemon,
stamping future possibilities
on my skull.

Outside, the light fades.
Squat hedges enclose the courtyard
like dwarf mourners
exiled from these halls of knowledge.
Listen! They spread rumours of a death.
What does infinity know? It is guarded and quiet.
What have we wedded to in these silent hours?
Whose night was this now over,
whose dark morn do we enter?

The *Museo della Scienza e della Tecnologia* is dedicated to the work of artist and scientist Leonardo da Vinci. Located in Milan, Italy, it houses models of some of da Vinci's most famous inventions.

New Song/Old Rag and Bone

I am shedding
rags   of skin
remnants of sun's disaster
brave Icarus, survived his fall

this parchment me
peeling from shoulders, chest
            dissolving
while new me emerges
stretched over skeleton
of the old, new
emotions
rise and fly off

I stand, take a breath
a wing breaks through
there   just below the
shoulder
                  blade
gleaming, new
appendage

misshapen, unfolding
glow of rain on skin
moves in quiet circles
            while above

the rooks yawl and clatter
towering on roof and
                    door

            below, I, glistening
rise and follow this
            trembling
nerve   flesh
            hollow bone
touch   tasting
      wind

Urban Density

looking in windows
I see pieces of myself
scattered in the glass

people
eating sandwiches, green salads
steaks appearing sudden on plates
bits of me sticking
to lips wiped clean

the breakfast special till 2 p.m.
I'll be the ham and eggs please
bite into a stranger sometime

in the knitting supplies store window
I lie crumpled in a ball of yarn
unhappy at being unfurled
over the loose box of needles
projecting outward

at the whim of some art college
window decorator

in the subway
green slime of ectoplasm
left behind on the last platform

blobs limply after the train
the old Chinese couple
woman ten paces behind the man
did I catch on her hat
shards of skin
wafting in the wind behind

in the trees
my hair catching like floss
hangs from the branches
city living

can be such a drag

Douglas at Dante's

*(For Douglas Valentine LePan, 1914-1998, soldier, teacher,
bureaucrat, poet, author, father, lover, friend)*

It was a surprising end to a new friendship,
like playing hide-and-seek with someone
who was never found again.

      Like lurching
down a street in a dream to find you'd
already gone, a treasure chest closed
forever. You, who were always so young seeming,
though your battle-wracked body belied
the fact, with its threat of strokes like a land
prone to earthquakes, while teaching me to be
something like youthful, who had never been so.

      An old man with a bent, sick body but
a young man's heart and mind, a friend like no
other—yes, no other—who were always
around for the call or a good laugh, a
surprising thought that illuminated
my mind with a lightning flash or an
unexpected curse ("Oh, for fuck's sakes!") from that
twisted mouth with its sly grin, rejoicing
at having upset the conversational
tone yet again.

How you would exclaim
at some grievance or other between thoughtful
observances on Pound or Eliot
(your "Tom"), as during that dinner
at Dante's, where you deemed it
"appropriate" that we should rendezvous
(of all places!)

    Yet on
arriving in the cool darkness of the
interior, amid those cobbled streets, I saw you
were right—it was no oddity to be
sitting with you on the far side of
the Atlantic, no pretension in the
invitation, just citizens of the world
taking our respective places in
Dante's café, who might once
have sat in those same seats
with Hemingway or poor mad Ezra.

    Somehow you made it seem
as though we belonged there amid the ruins
of your splendid past, I no more a stranger
than you, who had liberated such places
as these half a century earlier.

I see now it was my own Tuscan Villa,
as I sat listening to your stories
with fascination—the war, history, literature,
all entwining as one—while I ate
the suggested osso bucco, ("Yes, it's
very good, isn't it? Have some more wine.")
savouring each delightful bite as now
I savour your memory.

Winter Garden

(Lines written in the Giardini Pubblici, Milan, Italy)

these lovers on the grass
he lying, she whispering next to him
about the greenness of life
the granaries full of grain

don't they see the vines curling above them
arteries emptying abruptly
the dreadful arching of leaves
all around them

can't they hear the wind shrieking
the clouds to a bitter autumn
and know how soon at the window
they will howl when winter comes

Portrait of a Disaster

In this gallery the patrons stare
at my running shoes—purple Sisley.
They ignore the faces of history,

portraits rehearsed from another age
extracted through centuries of dirt,
war and neglect.

They stare and stare, as though I,
oracle from another world,
will offer them grace, hope

or opportunity.
Not I to look at, but these
sacred ones above—parts missing,

pieces gone astray—pietàs of history.
These are the faces of love,
more holy than

the bodies of saints,
surviving hate, death and more.
My shoes! My shoes! It is a crime,

a plague of the first rank.
I stare in return; their smiles
weaken as they turn away.

Is the inquisition over yet?
And is it decided—am I
to be burned or stoned or spared?

My hair, a Medusa's nest of sleeplessness,
mimics the faces on these walls.
It can't be helped! It can't be helped!

See what ages past lived in those eyes
where darkness now invades.
What pleasures were worn on that face

where grief now crowns this brow?
Whose heart did it belong to once,
whose warm hands?

Zero Hour

(*Lines written at the Prodi di Morivione, a war monument in Milan, Italy*)

Midnight, the toll slinks.
The sad lady has struck again,
leaving her vase full of remorse
and pale remembrances
in the garden bed
at the *Prodi di Morivione.*

Seventeen flowers and six vases
for twenty-three lost sons.
The candles burn,
cable buses pass in the street.
Silk tears fall on a plaster Madonna,
hands so cold, her child
a doll of clear pink plastic.
What sounds fill the air,
what angry cries
to mourn these leftover warriors?
I walk in silence among forgotten shadows,
without hope or a belief in the hereafter.
This is her demise,
theirs was eons ago.
Ours will come with candles—
seven veils and a tongue of flames.

Twenty-three faces—lost sons.
Dark glass, cold water.
Empty.

Flames burn, orange pygmies
dancing brightly in a cup.
Nightly I listen for stars and bells
labouring the hour. None come
to resurrect us and drown the morn.
The Madonna listens.
She eats her dead like candy,
drinking them into her body.
I wait in a bed of fire, mouth like a door.

Fruit

How does the fat peach
at the end of summer
feel in the final moments,
the surrender it's born for,
at the bite?

Violated, yet not destroyed
or incalculably ruined,
but resurrected at last,
ecstatic, filled with love
for the all.

ACKNOWLEDGEMENTS

Some of these pieces were previously published in the following
journals: *The New Quarterly, Canadian Literature, (EX)CITE
Journal of Contemporary Writing, Paperplates, Maple Tree Supple-
ment, The Prairie Journal of Canadian Literature, Ariel, LiNQ,
The White Rose, Ammonite, Nexus,* and *I Found It at the Movies*
(Ruth Pierson, ed.).

"Postcards from India" was inspired by a reading of *Meeting the
Buddha* (Molly Aitken, ed.) and a viewing of the restrospective
Y E S YOKO ONO at the Art Gallery of Ontario.

I offer my humble thanks to Halli Villegas, Tightrope's editor and
founder, for her heroic and visionary efforts to document what
might otherwise remain the obscure renderings of writers like
me. I also extend thanks to Jim Nason for bringing Tightrope to
my attention, to Keith Garebian for his help with the manuscript
proper, to Deanna Janovski for her crackerjack copy-editing skills,
and to Dawn Rae Downton who, though my contemporary, has
been my only true writing mentor, at least among the living, and
who was witness to the birth of the earliest of these pieces.

Leslieville, Toronto
Christmas morning, 2013

Jeffrey Round is a writer, director and composer. His most recent novel, *Lake On The Mountain*, won a Lambda Award in 2013. His short film *My Heart Belongs To Daddy* won an award for Best Canadian Director. His suite of songs, "Flowers for Aña Calil", was written for and recorded by soprano Lilac Caña. Jeffrey directed the Toronto production of Agatha Christie's *The Mousetrap*, the world's longest-running stage show. He has written for CBC and HGTV, among others. *In the Museum of Leonardo da Vinci* is his first poetry collection.